Elephant
vs.
Rhinoceros

Isabel Thomas

Raintree is an imprint of Capstone Global Library Limited, a company incorporated in England and Wales having its registered office at 264 Banbury Road, Oxford, OX2 7DY – Registered company number: 6695582

www.raintree.co.uk
myorders@raintree.co.uk

Edited by Penny McLoughlin
Designed by Steve Mead
Picture research by Svetlana Zhurkin
Production by Katy LaVigne
Printed and bound in India.

ISBN 978 1 474 74451 5 (hardback)
21 20 19 18 17
10 9 8 7 6 5 4 3 2 1

ISBN 978 1 474 74455 3 (paperback)
22 21 20 19 18
10 9 8 7 6 5 4 3 2 1

British Library Cataloguing in Publication Data
A full catalogue record for this book is available from the British Library.

Acknowledgements
We would like to thank the following for permission to reproduce photographs: Dreamstime: James Robins, 10; iStockphoto: guenterguni, 20, 22 (bottom left); Minden Pictures: Mary McDonald, 9, 22 (top left); Shutterstock: Andrea Izzotti, 13, digi-dreamgrafix, 11, Donovan van Staden, 16, 22 (bottom right), EcoPrint, 15, 22 (middle right), Eduard Kyslynskyy, 18, Four Oaks, 17, gualtiero boffi, 5, 21, Jez Bennett, back cover (right), 6, 22 (top right), JMx Images, cover (left), Johan Swanepoel, 19, john michael evan potter, 12, nale (silhouette), 6, 7, nelik, 7, 22 (middle left), pashabo (texture), cover and throughout, Sergey Uryadnikov, 8, Simon Eeman, cover (right), Villiers Steyn, back cover (left), 14, Volodymyr Burdiak, 4

Every effort has been made to contact copyright holders of material reproduced in this book. Any omissions will be rectified in subsequent printings if notice is given to the publisher.

All the Internet addresses (URLs) given in this book were valid at the time of going to press. However, due to the dynamic nature of the Internet, some addresses may have changed, or sites may have changed or ceased to exist since publication. While the author and publisher regret any inconvenience this may cause readers, no responsibility for any such changes can be accepted by either the author or the publisher.

Some words are shown in bold, **like this**.
You can find them in the glossary on page 22.

Contents

Meet the animals 4

Size and strength 6

Speed..8

Brain power 10

Survival skills..12

Super senses...14

Deadly weapons 16

Fighting skills..18

Who wins? 20

Picture glossary 22

Find out more..23

Index...24

Meet the animals

What has big ears and a long **trunk**?
It's the **African elephant**.

What has a large horn and thick skin?

It's the
white rhino.

Would an elephant or a rhino win in a fight?
Let's find out!

Size and strength

An elephant's enormous size means it can reach fruit that is high in the treetops. It can even push trees over to get at the juiciest leaves.

This is how tall an elephant is next to a human.

This is how tall a rhino is next to a human.

A rhino has a huge hump of **muscle** on its back. It uses this to move its massive head. Its tough lips are designed for tearing large mouthfuls of grass.

Speed

An elephant walks along at a slow pace, but can cover big distances. It will charge to escape danger or scare an enemy.

A rhino may look clumsy, but it can run as fast as a **galloping** horse! It can run for longer than an elephant can.

Brain power

An elephant can easily remember the best places to find food. It is good at learning how to use tools. Some elephants use branches to swat flies away.

A rhino is not as clever as an elephant. Though some rhinos have been known to open gates or car doors with their top lip!

Survival skills

It's hot under the African sun. An elephant uses its giant ears to cool down. It can flap them to make a breeze. Warm blood loses heat as it flows through the ears.

A rhino keeps cool by wallowing in mud. A thick layer of mud keeps the sun off its skin. If water dries up, a rhino can last up to four days without water.

Super senses

Sharp senses help plant eaters to find food. They are also important for avoiding enemies. An elephant will sniff the air with its **trunk** for signs of danger.

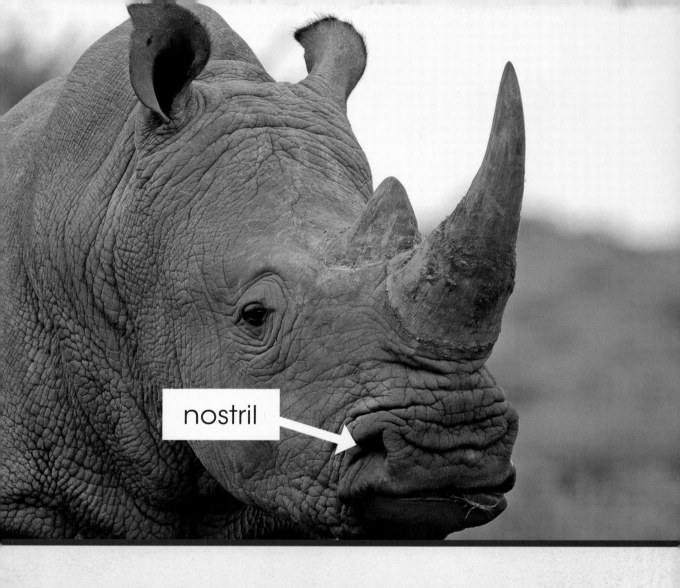

nostril

Look at the rhino's big **nostrils**. That's a
clue to show it has a great sense of smell.
A rhino cannot see very well, but it can
twist its ears around to hear sounds better.

Deadly weapons

An elephant's **tusks** are made of **ivory**. This is much tougher than rhino horn. Each tusk can weigh the same as two children!

A rhino has two horns on top of its head.
They are made of the same material
as our fingernails. The horns wear down
easily and can even break off in a fight!

Fighting skills

Male elephants fight to show who is stronger and attract females. They wrestle with their **trunks** and **tusks** until the weaker male backs down.

Male rhinos get angry if they see another large male nearby. They stand nose to nose and stare at each other until the weaker rhino runs away.

Who wins?

What would happen if an elephant fought a rhino? The animals would charge towards each other, using their **tusks** or horns as a weapon.

But who would win?

	Elephant	Rhino
Size	10	8
Strength	10	9
Speed	6	9
Energy	5	8
Brains	10	6
Senses	8	8
Defence	10	7
Weapons	9	8
Fighting skills	9	9
Attack	9	7
TOTAL	**86/100**	79/100

ELEPHANT WINS!

Picture glossary

gallop run fast

ivory a hard, white material

muscle a part of the body that causes movement

nostril an opening in the nose for breathing and smelling

trunk the long nose of an elephant

tusk a long, curved, pointed tooth that sticks out of the mouth

Find out more

Books

Elephants (Animal Lives), Sally Morgan
(QED Publishing, 2014)

Elephants (Wildlife Animals Encyclopedia for Kids),
(Baby iQ Builder Books, 2016)

Elephants Are Awesome! (Awesome African
Animals!), Martha E.H. Rustad (Raintree, 2015)

Websites

www.bbc.co.uk/newsround/37442236
Watch a video on 11 things you never knew about
elephants.

**www.savetherhino.org/rhino_info/for_kids/get_
creative**
Get creative with these rhino activities.

**www.sciencekids.co.nz/sciencefacts/animals/
elephant.html**
Interesting facts about the biggest land mammal in
the world.

Index

charge 8, 20

ears 4, 12, 15

fight 5, 17, 18-19, 20

horns 5, 16-17, 20

humps 7

ivory 16

lips 7, 11

muscles 7

nostrils 15

run 9, 19

senses 14-15

tools 10

trunks 4, 14, 18

tusks 16, 18, 20

wallow 13

water 13

wrestle 18